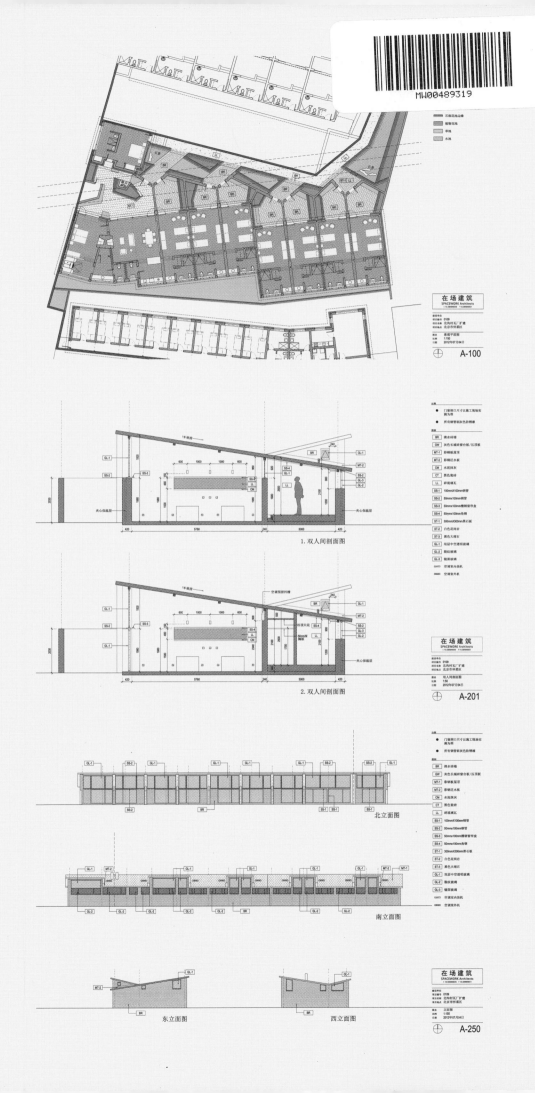

GREAT WALL STYLE
Building Home with Jim Spear

images
Publishing

GREAT WALL STYLE

Building Home with Jim Spear

By Tessa Cheek

Photography by Robert McLeod

Published in Australia in 2013 by
The Images Publishing Group Pty Ltd
ABN 89 059 734 431
6 Bastow Place, Mulgrave, Victoria 3170, Australia
Tel: +61 3 9561 5544 Fax: +61 3 9561 4860
books@imagespublishing.com
www.imagespublishing.com

Copyright © The Images Publishing Group Pty Ltd. 2013
The Images Publishing Group Reference Number: 1100

National Library of Australia Cataloguing-in-Publication entry

Author: Cheek, Tessa, author.

Title: Great Wall style: building home with Jim Spear / Tessa Cheek; Jim Spear.

ISBN: 978 1 86470 563 8 (hardback)

Subjects: Spear, Jim.
                    Architecture—China—20th century.
                    Architecture—China—21st century.
                     Architecture—China—20th century—Pictorial works.
                    Architecture—China—21st century—Pictorial works.

Dewey Number: 720.951

Edited by Mandy Herbet

Designed by The Graphic Image Studio Pty Ltd, Mulgrave, Australia
www.tgis.com.au

Pre-publishing services by United Graphic Pte Ltd., Singapore

Printed on 150gsm Quatro Silk Matt by Everbest Printing Co. Ltd., in Hong Kong/China

IMAGES has included on its website a page for special notices in relation to this and our other publications. Please visit www.imagespublishing.com.

Contents

Foreword

Design can serve as a kind of alchemy. A carefully placed window draws you out and away and can also offer a surprising connection. An object pulls you into the story of its making. A small new building can lead to a fresh reading of the much older buildings around it.

This sort of magic is well represented in these pages. But it's important to consider a perhaps rarer project — the intellectual and creative depth with which Jim Spear has defined where and how he works.

In the vastness of China, swells of urbanization are already transforming a built environment that has been mostly rural for thousands of years. A startled vanguard of architects is starting to look, yet again, to the countryside and its ideas — the same place and locus of imbedded intelligence that Jim's been working in and learning from for the last 19 years. Over that span of time, he has built a life, a body of work and a design method within the limits of three adjacent villages. The mesh of those projects has offered him intimate introductions to all scales of village life and engaged him in everything from legal and social structures to construction materials and habits of building.

This hasn't been distance learning or produced the kind of abstract — historically, often dangerous — lessons that come from theorizing about some place you understand best on paper. Each of Jim's 30 houses to date has been built under the tutelage of an older building, with locally sourced materials and in partnership with village construction crews. Working within the limits of the northern Chinese courtyard house typology — as defined along this Beijing stretch of the Great Wall — he has been able to run a series of experiments on its formal possibilities. In one case, a glass pavilion occupies the center of the courtyard space. On another site, the new design is completely hidden within the untouched shell of a particularly fine-boned farmhouse. Elsewhere, it's mostly in the different flutter of the roofline that you see his touch. Everywhere, new design is understood as catalyzing a conversation with what has long stood in the same place.

From this 20-years-in vantage point, it is not clear to what extent Jim's bigger project was in the cards from the start and to what extent it only revealed itself slowly, in incremental payoffs for time invested. Whatever the strategy, it qualifies Jim Spear as a member of a very exclusive club. Village life is known to be hard to crack anywhere. In China, there have been very few foreigners comfortable enough with the language to put down deep roots. In Jim's case, there is ease in so many of the vocabularies — material, conversational and cultural — of the three-village territory he has made home. The hat trick is that his work in this place is anything but a footnote. It is integrated and quiet enough to have become part of its existing grain and innovative enough to offer a plausible model for its future.

Amy Lelyveld

Little Windows

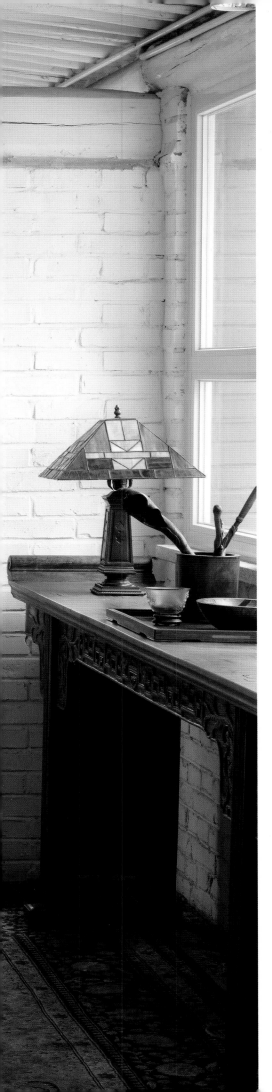

The window is small and square. No more than half a meter wide, it's set high enough in the study's west wall that the view is straight on. Adjacent to the much larger north-facing window opposite Jim Spear's desk, this imaginative portal is an oddity. It draws the eye again and again to a shifting canvas. Seated, the view in early winter is of Mutianyu's clear sky. Stand up and the window frames the tiled roof of a woodshed and a nearby mountain range defined by its profile formation — the Sleeping Buddha.

Jim's desk, built from a salvaged door, was a gift from his wife and business partner, Tang Liang. Behind the desk, Jim installed a set of shelves to present and enjoy an idiosyncratic collection. Some 20 rectangular glass mirrors punctuate a display of craft pieces and reflect, like a series of small framed windows, what the north window actually opens wide to: the facade of the farmhouse next door which Jim added as a wing containing an apartment for the family's live-in couple, Liang's fabric workroom and a guest suite. Above this wing rises the broad face of the mountain with its crenelated crown — the Great Wall.

Jim is a collector of material stories, views from all manner of small windows. Even a pocket-sized, carved wooden object can be like a window. For Jim, these, or slightly larger boxes and trays, all offer particular views. Some hold letters and plans, others paperclips and bits of discarded art glass. Yet they also open into memory. Through the patina of use, they reveal the story of their long life. As the conversational collection of a self-taught architect, they anchor Jim's personal story and creative process.

"See this?" Jim says, turning a square tray in his hands. "Someone carved this from a single piece of wood. These four corners? *Almost* identical curves. They came from someone's craft and practice, so they're not quite square. That's why it's valuable. The maker's hand lives in a skilled imperfection, an implicit signature."

In this study where Jim sketches and reviews plans, he has surrounded himself with myriad small windows. Mirrors reflect Jim's home, the village of Mutianyu, and the shift of light and season playing over the many faces of the Great Wall. Wooden boxes and trays, even a Ming brush pot carved from a single branch of rosewood, or *huanghuali*, all carry a material connection between Jim and the craft as well as the people who inspire him.

"What I remember with my collections," Jim writes, "is frequently who bought the piece and gave it to me, or where I found it together with Liang or a friend."

A Maldivian coconut tray, from his daughter Lauren. A fantastical wooden monster, brightly painted, a gift from his sister. A handblown glass bowl Jim and Liang discovered in Murano. Each object tells the relational history of a life ongoing and offers a testament to the memory of material — a principle which guides and stirs Jim as he designs. Ultimately, the collection itself provides a view not just into Jim's creative practice but also into his personal story, the discovery and creation of the home.

Left: Clear north light fills the library and Jim's adjacent study. This lean-to structure was added when Jim converted his Mutianyu hut to a full-time home, providing views of a private courtyard garden and the Great Wall cresting the nearby mountain ridge. He believes "a good home is never finished" and both these spaces have since been re-envisioned.

Left: Jim's redesigned library with energy-efficient LED ceiling lights and handcrafted walnut bookshelves. Double-paned glass is fitted into the trapezoidal openings above the beam to provide sound privacy in Jim's study. As I explored the library, I found that many of the books in his idiosyncratic collection were marked with the phrase, "return eventually to Jim," in the front cover.

Above: The little window in Jim's study set off by a polished rock crystal from Fujian.

Right: Jim's study pre-remodel. Collected mirrors on the south wall reflect ambient light. When Jim is seated at the work counter in front of them, they offer snatches of scenes from around the room, the garden and the Great Wall. Other treasures — rosewood and sandalwood boxes, carved trays and water ewers for a scholar's desk — are carefully intermingled among the ever-present mirrors, Jim's little windows.

Below: Jim's study post-remodel, still filled with mirrors. Jim keeps this broad worktable for sketching, conversing with guests and luxuriating in the moment. The calligraphy *wanfeng* means evening wind and was given to Jim by a Chinese friend for his birthday in 1981.

When I first began to interview Jim about his work, I knew little about the history of China and even less about architecture. From the start, it was clear I had a lot of self-teaching to do, a process Jim knew well. But the first book he recommended seemed to have nothing to do with the designing and building of homes. It was *The Memory Palace of Matteo Ricci*. The renowned China historian Jonathan Spence tells the story of the Renaissance-era Jesuit missionary who, at the end of the 16th century, brought with him to China a Western mnemonic device called the memory palace. The device was twofold. The well-known first step required simply associating an idea with an image or imaginary object. The second mental maneuver, one which has fascinated Jim in relation to his design work, was to build a house for that memory image.

Imagine a pewter liquor pot you have endowed with a memory of your wife laughing on a Sunday morning. Place it in a corridor, on the uppermost glass shelf across from a south-facing window. Here it is home.

With its fluted neck and brass handle, your Sunday morning pot is particular but also one of many. It lives on a wall of glass shelves running the length of the sunny corridor. Reminiscences about your wife coexist with a vast collection of pewter vessels. Likewise, a stout teapot calls to mind a journey to the Grand Canyon with your father. A pewter cup engraved with a poetic drinking song was a gift from

Opposite: Jim's collection of pewter liquor pots originated with his interest in their shapes and silhouettes. Over a quarter century, with enthusiastic help from Liang, the pewter collection has grown to include representative teapots, oil pots, water vessels, cups, trays, boxes, vases, urns and altar candlesticks. The pewter ranges from the imperial to the vernacular and many of the pieces are displayed here on one-of-a-kind wooden stands that had outlived the precious objects they were originally carved to hold.

Below: Jim and Liang on the Mutianyu Great Wall with their village as a backdrop.

the wife of Chalmers Johnson, your professor and mentor, after he passed away. If you are Jim, you can drink from it lessons learned during your days as a graduate student at Berkeley. This is the eccentric, unfolding magic of the memory palace. The corridor, the whole house for memory, lives, breathes and is open to renovation and expansion over time. All the device requires is a simple faith in the power of a particular object to shelter remembrance, its capacity as a small window.

By the time Father Ricci made the long journey from Italy to China, the Great Wall at Mutianyu had stood, and crumbled, for a thousand years. It was under renovation, a process that took nearly three centuries. In stony valleys all along the granite barricade, thousands of builders founded a string of small villages. In Mutianyu, these new residents cut terraced orchards into the hillsides and reinforced each level with a dry-stone skirt wall. The rest of the "trash rock" salvaged from would-be croplands found its way into the foundations of stone farmhouses.

Nineteen-eighty-six saw the completion of the most recent major renovation of the Mutianyu Great Wall, this time as a historical landmark and tourist destination. That same year, Jim moved to China. He'd left a doctoral program in Political Science at the University of California, Berkeley, when he realized that what he really wanted was a career and life, wholly based in China, not just sojourns for academic research. By then fluent in Chinese, Jim found a promising position in Beijing with a respected pioneer in joint ventures and settled into a tiny apartment with Tang Liang and their newly born daughter. He also made his first visit to the Mutianyu stretch of the Great Wall and the small village that shares the site's name.

Over the intervening years, Jim returned often to visit the Wall at Mutianyu. He had fallen for the village, a community of roughly 200 households where many earned their living from the chestnut orchards covering the surrounding hillsides. In those days, stalls and stores at the base of the Wall already sold an array of desirable goods. New cloisonné, embroidery and carvings joined the locally grown dried

Below: Many of the homes Jim designs, such as *Pavilion* or *Red Door*, begin as abandoned and dilapidated huts like this one in Mutianyu Village.

Opposite: The first house Jim was commissioned to renovate is paved inside and out with the same kind of bricks used to renovate sections of the Great Wall. Five bays are now combined as a single expansive living space, with a door cut at the far end to a converted hay shed — now a kitchen with a small window overlooking the valley.

persimmons and an influx of factory-made souvenirs. On one visit, Jim discovered an antique sapphire ring that he bought from a local merchant as a present for Liang. A few years later, the couple would acquire something much larger.

Jim and Liang became permanent residents of Mutianyu thanks to a serendipitous meeting with Li Fengquan, a villager and vendor at the Great Wall. Walking down the path from the site in the early 1990s, Jim fell into conversation with Li. Writing of it years later, Jim recalls the moment vividly. "I said, 'I am sorry, I'm not interested in buying a souvenir today, but I have to tell you I envy you living in such a beautiful place near the Great Wall. I have always dreamed of being able to have a home here, but I don't think I'll ever be able to manage it.' Out of the blue, this Chinese peasant said, 'I'll help you'."

Just a few weeks later, Li helped the couple sign a long-term lease on a traditional village farmhouse. It wouldn't be long before Jim began to tinker with the structure.

The house stands high on the steep eastern face of Mutianyu valley. Its rough courtyard, formed by a series of tied-together bushes, then featured a pigsty and a huge dog. The house itself had unusually high walls, bearing the promise of higher ceilings. It had been built by the mayor's brother for their father, who, in his advanced age, retired to the home of one son.

"For years," Jim recalls, "he would walk back up to his old house and visit us there. He liked to sit and be with the house, to see how it had changed. He was a kind man."

The first round of renovations turned the farmhouse into a cozy escape from the hectic corporate world Jim's family and friends inhabited in Beijing. Julie Upton-Wang, a fellow Beijing expat and now a local business partner with Jim and Liang, remembers those early days fondly. With neither internet nor cellphone service, she and Jim would often spend an entire day playing Scrabble.

In 2005, at 50, Jim had a mid-life crisis. After almost 20 years in business, it was time for a personal renovation. Envisioning a quiet country life, days spent pottering around the garden and making small, tasteful adjustments to his farmhouse, Jim cashed in his chips and moved to Mutianyu full-time. Despite this vision, he was far from retiring. Having turned the family's country house into a permanent home, Jim found that it became so popular with their circle that friends and acquaintances began to ask for help securing and redesigning their own village farmhouses. Within the year, Jim set to work designing a house for a friend just down the hill.

Not long after he and Liang became real villagers, Jim was approached by the mayor of Mutianyu, who explained that the village was rapidly losing residents and badly in need of local enterprise. Partnering with their close friend Julie and her husband, Peiming Wang, Jim and Liang leased the vacant village schoolhouse and renovated it as a local foods restaurant and glass-blowing workshop. The first of several sustainable tourism enterprises, The Schoolhouse opened in 2006 and is now one of the area's largest sources of local employment.

Today, an eco-retreat, three restaurants and dozens of houses later, Jim describes his process by citing Matteo Ricci's culture-bridging mental architecture. Working long hours at his desk surrounded by a variety of small windows, Jim has designed and built a memory palace for each home by hyper-endowing objects and spaces with meaning. There could be no more apt creative process for a designer who roots his projects in vernacular traditions and existing village buildings.

A house that has stood for 50, 100, even 200 years already embodies the first step of Ricci's memory device. Time has moved in everywhere and memory has seeped into the structure's bones. Sometimes, in the process of stripping the crumbling *torchis* —

Opposite: The peasant house at the heart of Jim's own home was opened end-to-end and painted entirely in white, black and gray. The bones are old but this living space is starkly modern, warmed by a roaring fire and colorful art.

Above: This six-panel folding screen, 2.75 meters high, was carved in solid hardwood during the early Qing Dynasty. It forms the backdrop in Jim's master bedroom.

a mixture of straw and mud — from an interior wall, Jim finds himself standing in a room built of pillaged bricks, portions of the Great Wall hauled down from the ridgeline. Ceilings, dropped low by paper spanned over bamboo frames, are removed to expose the space above. In the kitchen, where the ceilings are unpapered to stave off fire, Jim preserves the rafters' patina — a black coating left by decades of cooking smoke. Often a portion of the family room's stone wall is also scorched where the built-in daybed, the *kang*, once stood and was warmed by the flue from the kitchen fire.

At night, these images linger stubbornly in his mind's eye, traces of an ineffable material memory. The rest of the home, the new and renovated portions, Jim builds like a memory palace to house what already stands. Everywhere the past rises up, a physical beginning, but also a constraint not unlike the inherited rules of formal poetry.

"People always forget that it's really free-verse that's most difficult," Jim tells me. "That this poet has to invent their vernacular out of nothing, out of whole cloth. It's much harder to say something meaningful to a vacuum than it is to respond to a limit — a meter, a rhyme scheme or a charred-up stone wall."

As with formal verse, the boundaries set by stone walls, blackened roof beams and latticed windows provide — actually define — an ample space for innovation and even play. Just as Ricci's Memory Palace allows for renovation and expansion over time, so Jim's design aims to limn a storied space to the possibility of new lives and new narratives; to build a home as suited for contemporary life as it is for sheltering the history of lives lived.

Before a house's plans are drawn up, Jim drifts off to sleep each night picturing possible views through its windows, projecting the vivid house-to-be on his closed eyelids. Before daybreak, he wakes up to sketch this dream of a home as a tentative plan. Though his own house is still tucked in shadow, dawn tints the Great Wall pink and then gold as he formalizes the design. Gradually, the study fills with clear northern light. A dog barks. Muffled voices. Clangs from the kitchen.

One of the first projects I toured with Jim was a recently completed country home made from a farmhouse in Tianxianyu, a village nearby Mutianyu. Light enters this house's new great room through multiple windows. Over the course of the day, the sun streams in through first one and then the other of the open pediments at the room's east and west poles. It's unheard of to make windows of the gables in a Chinese farmhouse. These windows allow a person standing on the adjoining rooftop terrace to look right through the house, end to end. But more than that, a terrace lounger will see through this pair of windows to a framed view exclusively of mountain and sky. Jim walked carefully through the lines of sight in his mind's eye and raised wall heights to insure this elevated seclusion for both resident and neighbor without sacrificing views of the landscape.

A clerestory runs the length of the great room's south wall, which backs onto the village alley. High enough to ensure privacy without window coverings, the opening is sheltered from the hot sun in the summer, but admits an abundance of warm yellow light in winter — a heartfelt welcome to natural light as well as an energy-saver that Jim picked up from the traditional vernacular. In a complete departure from those regional customs, the great room faces north with a wall of windows entirely open to the courtyard, to the facade of the house's original structure and to the craggy mountain range, its towering contours improbably capped by the Great Wall. Finally, a small window cuts the east wall of the great room. The first light of the day filters through this portal, which is just a hand's width across, though nearly 2 meters tall.

Jim speaks quietly. Perhaps it's shyness that pushes him back in his chair as he says, "I like to think of those windows as my paintings."

Above: One of Jim's small windows, located in the dressing room of his Mutianyu home's master suite. He chose this view and proportion based on the long tradition of Chinese scroll paintings that often feature landscapes and attenuated lines like those of a tree branch. "Every time you look, this scene has repainted itself," Jim observes.

Opposite: A light-filled reading nook projects from *Big Rock House's* living room. The angled courtyard wall ensures just enough privacy.

Top: Outside and inside in harmony: The building plot for the farmhouse Jim leased was terraced from the mountainside. This heavy stone wall holds the mountain back. The unusual post-and-beam structure shown here allowed for a connecting tile roofline when a new wing was added.

Above: Even the Great Wall cannot defend against time. This watchtower near Mutianyu crumbles into earth and tree roots snake between ancient bricks.

Right: In *Eagle's Rest*, Jim juxtaposes at a right angle to the old farmhouse a new glass house of similar dimensions. "Even a glass house is an enclosed space, a volume. How do you light that volume? How do you keep it from becoming a void?" he asks. Here expansive views to the south fill the pavilion with warm light. The room is anchored by a sculptural, freestanding kitchen and hearth built from Great Wall bricks salvaged when another peasant dwelling was renovated.

Above: Little windows in *Mumanyu* provide bursts of light and snatches of views in the kitchen. The gable window complements a skylight. This room, which is actually small and low at the ceiling, thus feels airy and open.

Opposite top: Stripped to the essentials: *Mumanyu's kang* room reveals the rough brickwork and rafters of the original dwelling. The glass in the round window Jim cut into the solid west wall is, on the outside, actually set in a larger, square frame. This nod to the neighbor downhill, who objected strongly to a round window, became a valued feature.

Opposite bottom: "The almost instinctive parsimony of poor people — never throw anything away — can lead to an oddly picturesque squalor," says Jim. "One should never mistake the endurance of poverty as a perverse liking for it. These are real working villages, not folk museums for urbanites, occupied by real working people, not actors putting on a show."

Above: What is real and what is reflected? Here, the new great room in *Heart's Desire* was shot from under the eaves of the old house. Because of the structure's asymmetrical roof, the window wall seems to disappear into the sky and we see right through the south clerestory to greenery. The reflected image, offset by the pear tree in the courtyard, is actually the same view as seen from within the great room — the untouched façade of the original house backdropped by the ridgeline and Great Wall.

In the Valley by the Wall

n October, the sky turns up celadon in the evening, the color of a good teacup. Standing on the Great Wall, the view is of the Yanshan Mountains rising blue and jagged over the valleys. All along the barricade, deciduous trees have rooted themselves in the rammed earth foundations and sprouted between cracks in the massive bricks. They flush red and orange, consuming the Wall in leafy fire. Below, the valleys uncurl like tributaries of a high stone river, each ravine neatly appointed with a village.

A dirt track connects the village of Mutianyu to Beigou and Tianxianyu. It winds up steep hillsides and splits along terraced orchards. At the crest of a ridge between two villages, the path widens as if to pause, overlooking the whole dusky sweep of the valley. At this height, a few of the old crown pines still stand guard. Not long ago, these trees covered the hillsides. As an outsider, you can easily lose your way and wander north into steeper climbs, even to the Wall itself. Yet once the path is known it shows itself for what it is: the simplest, quickest line of connection between villagers and their chestnut trees, between their homes and those of a friend or a neighbor.

Left: Many towers like this one filled with its own bricks stand watch over the skein of villages under the Wall. According to Great Wall chronicler William Lindesay, many of Chairman Mao's proclamations, including "Let the past serve the present," and "Smash the four olds," encouraged residents to harvest everything from bricks to old wooden doors and historic plaques. Often stolen bricks can be found as load-bearing walls in village homes — a patrimony dispersed.

Following pages: Photographer Robert McLeod climbed the rugged mountains near Mutianyu to capture these vertiginous Great Wall images, bringing armchair visitors into the stunning setting that captivated and inspired Jim.

A smell like burnt sugar arrives in November and clings to everything — scarf and fingertip, the wrappers of candied hawthorn and leaves of cabbage from the local shop's cellar. It's coal-burning season in Northern China. Brown vines snake over courtyard walls and gourds hang like heavy ornaments 2 meters from the ground. The steep hillsides are littered with the spiny husks of chestnuts, like so many squashed sea urchins. All along the dry streambeds, fat golden persimmons fall from their unreachable top branches. Tang Liang brings a bagful picked from her garden to line the windowsills in The Schoolhouse courtyard. She spends the next week half shouting, half laughing as guests and staff alike snack on the luminous decorations, which taste of sweet carrot and tomato.

The cusp of a new season is Jim's favorite time for the view from his study window. "In the winter all you get is mountains," he says, looking out at the bare trees. The Wall above is whiter than bone. A few village chimneys send out their thin smoke signals — life at home, though not in the streets. The houses wrap themselves in blankets. The village goes quiet.

Opposite: In the room he designed to store and appreciate Tang Liang's textile collection, Jim mortared a rubble masonry wall with plain concrete. Later, a client requested a warmer cast for their stone walls, leading Jim to mix mud with the concrete, resulting in a tawny glow.

Left: A mid-Qing bed dressed with ethnic fabrics from Tang Liang's collection. The cracked ice pattern of this antique has served as a model for Jim when he designs roof and window lattices.

Above: The polished river stone chimney Jim added to the back of his farmhouse has now been enclosed by the lean-to of the library. The small screen or *pingfeng* on the table is from the early Qing dynasty. Its inscription reads, "The mountain is high and the water is silent."

In China, farmers plant things according to the traditional calendar...

立春 the beginning of Spring Feb. 4   清明 Pure Brightness Apr 5   立夏 —the beginning of Summer May 5
惊蛰 the waking of Insect March 5   谷雨 Grain Rain Apr 20   小满 lesser fullness of Grain May 21
春分   spring Equinox March 20   春雨惊春清谷天，夏满芒夏暑相连   芒种 Grain in Beard Jun 6
立秋 the beginning of Autumn Aug 8   秋处露秋寒霜降 冬雪雪冬小大寒   夏至   Summer Solstice Jun 21
处暑 the end of Heat Aug 23   小暑 lesser Heat July 7
白露 white Dew Sep. 8   霜降 Frost's Descent Oct 23   大暑 Greater Heat July 23
秋分   Autumn Equinox Sep 23   立冬 the beginning of winter Nov 7   冬至   Winter Solstice Dec 22
寒露 Cold Dew Oct. 8   小雪 lesser Snow Nov. 22   小寒 lesser Cold Jan. 6
                大雪 Greater Snow Dec. 7   大寒 Greater cold Jan. 20

Above: Classrooms at The Schoolhouse have been renovated into dining rooms which still retain their original blackboards. Photography stylist Ampol Paul J composed this arrangement of local produce in honor of The Schoolhouse's commitment to slow food.

Opposite: This gatehouse structure was built off the external wall of the village storeroom, making it impossible to incorporate the beams in the end wall. The iron column had been added when that beam proved too weak to hold up the roof. Jim highlighted the free-floating beam and the stone wall with a row of concealed LED lights. All that remains of the *kang* that once stood in this humble space is the char on the end wall.

"These are fresh local eggs," says Liang. "A neighbor brings them over. Once you taste them you really know what an egg is. Even their yolk is more yellow." She cooks them simply, first in a little oil, finished with a touch of butter. That's all they need. She sits down in the sunny breakfast nook Jim added to the house.

"When he first suggested we move out here full-time, I thought he was joking," Liang says, coffee steaming from a painted mug pressed between both palms. It's part of a collection she and Jim picked up in Italy. "I couldn't believe it. I told him, I'm not a peasant. To me it was an insult!" She laughs, then looks out the window across their formal garden and low courtyard wall to the face of the mountain formation known as the Sleeping Buddha.

"So yes, when we first started, my major challenge was having been a city person. Of course, during the Cultural Revolution we were all sent to the countryside, but that wasn't life. I had never really lived in a small village. I didn't understand — I still don't — how the peasants think. I'm still working on it. I'm always working on how to communicate, because I believe without it you have nowhere to begin."

Opposite: Take away the clutter and the clean lines of a cozy and functional home will stand out: hand-chiseled foundation stones, lozenges set gracefully in the heavy brick, wooden lattices, a sturdy end wall reaching out to eaves above.

Above: Jim preserved the facade of *Big Rock House* under a glass hallway. Its cheap but functional red brick and concrete window sills are offset with a beautiful wooden lattice.

Over many years, from negotiating their first lease on the home she sits in now to getting the final official seal, or chop, of more than 70 needed to begin work on The Schoolhouse Orchard, Liang has worked with Jim to lay each project's ineffable, and indispensable, foundation in building relationships.

"It took a long time to earn and build trust in the community," she says. "So we work to appreciate the people who have helped us along the way. You don't forget those people. You give them little gifts just to let them know you're thinking of them. In Chinese, we have this saying: 'Even a small gift is not too small. You can give someone a bag of sunflower seeds.' Which is to say, the small gift is vital. Just this fall, some of our neighbors came over with melons from their garden, the first of the harvest."

She smiles, takes a bite of omelet. "We live here. We get to eat these eggs!"

Opposite: Buildings all over the villages were constructed with harvested field stones to form "trash walls." Here, builders have reinforced the mortared stone construction with three tracks of fired bricks.

Above: Red brick painted gray by government fiat in Mutianyu. At center, iron doors have weathered to an almost textile patina.

Above: Xiaolumian on a foggy morning.

Above right: Fresh *kang* bricks, made by hand, temper in the afternoon sun.

Opposite: Golden light catches in the lattices and the hanging corn at Xiaolumian, the artisanal noodle shop Jim designed in Beigou. Corn became a staple in Northern China after it was introduced from North America in the 17th century.

It's hard to exaggerate the importance of relationships to building in a Chinese village. "These communities," explains Jim, "are full of traditional superstitions about how houses should be laid out, which way they should face, how they should speak to each other. Generally speaking that's a kind of *feng shui*, and villagers certainly think of it in that way. I've learned that if I don't pay attention to those principles it's much harder to build."

Inherited, yet subject to constant reinterpretation, *feng shui* guides the rural planning of any given village — albeit in a somewhat haphazard way. From the orchard path connecting Beigou to Mutianyu, both villages appear to be organized like the froth of a fast-moving mountain stream. Rowhouses pile up against each other with the abrupt intersections of flotsam. There's the eddy of the occasional formal courtyard. The surrounding orchards, terraces on terraces, echo like ripples up the valley.

This repetition of row house on row house has a large-scale organic quality, which comes from the *feng shui* injunction that a home must face south while still responding to its immediate surroundings — boulder, creek, orchard. In its fullest sense, *feng shui* guides the particularities of a given home's design, from garden to entryway to sleeping quarters.

"*Feng shui* has its attractions," says Jim. "The whole attention to views, to lines of sight. I mean, I love mirrors and one of the occasional principles in the villages is to use mirrors to scare away the devils. I use mirrors to bring in light and to open up spaces. Maybe it amounts to the same thing."

Opposite: *Denglong* holiday lanterns lend a festive air to *Xiaolumian's* preserved facade.

Above: "How you pave makes a huge difference, both indoors and out," notes Jim. "In this case, *Xiaolumian's* dining terrace adds year-round color and a connection to place. My local craftsmen laid a mixture of brick and stone fragments with remnants of Great Wall bricks."

Above: Jim converted this low building, once the village smithy, into a private dining room with its own fireplace. Outside, an old millstone stands on a grinding wheel, both from Jim and Liang's collection of hand-chiseled mills and feeding troughs.

Right: Builders left about half of this brick wall unmortared. The foundation — large stones placed directly on the earth and covered in a thin layer of concrete — has since settled.

Opposite: The weathered exterior of a farmhouse, captured by Robert McLeod who saw beauty in the dusty plastic burlap and earthen pot. The farmhouse doors are also crude, just single planks which pivot on pegs, less expensive than hinges on a carpentered door.

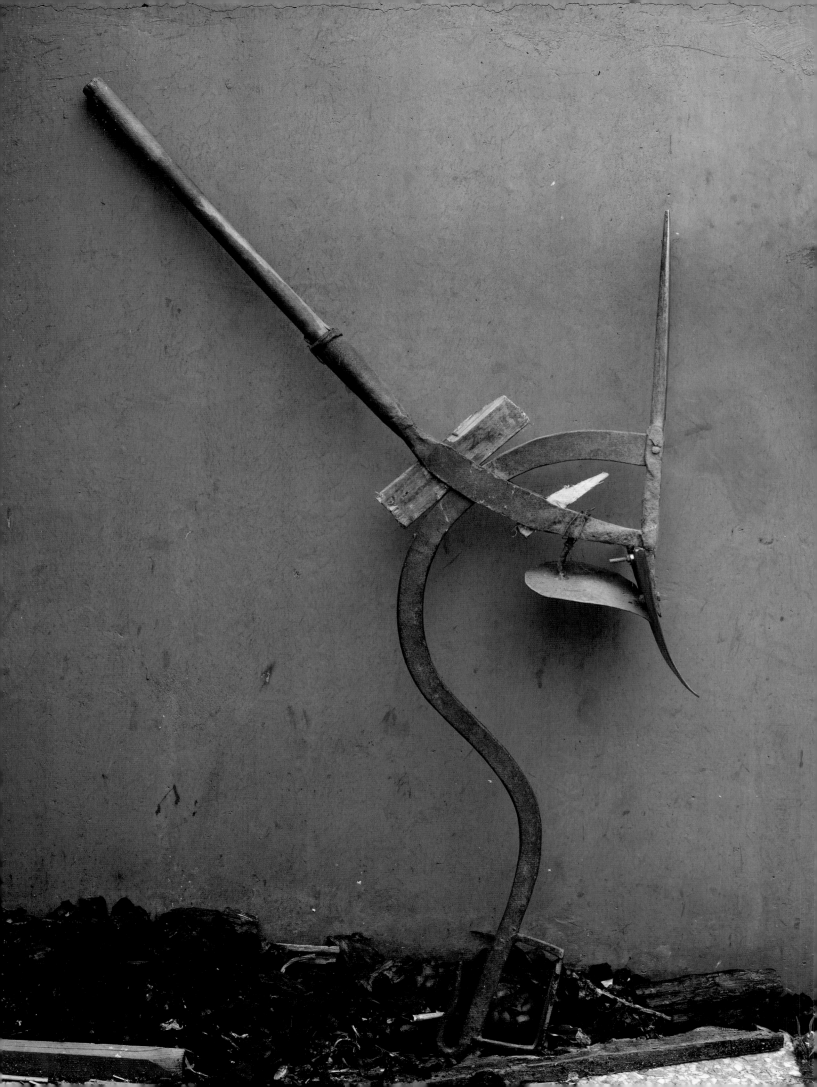

Opposite: Lumps of coal beneath the curves of an old plow. During winter, smoke from coal, leaf and husk fills the valleys and billows fog-like up the foothills.

Above: A bench that Jim commissioned for The Schoolhouse courtyard. "There's a furniture-making tradition in China that's similar to the Adirondack," he says. "The practice uses stumps and branches, perfects them and turns them into fine furniture. The craft subtly turns the crude into the refined."

Below: Kindling from pruned fruit trees and low branches of other trees, lopped off without harm. Nothing is wasted.

Opposite top: Late-blooming chrysanthemums overflow in luminous yellow along the roadside in Beigou village. The fall flowers are cultivated for their color and to make a soothing tisane.

Opposite bottom: This still life with basketry and a whisk broom newly bought from the village store shows the worm-eaten facade of *Grandma's Place* and the inexpensive fiberglass frames of the curtain window behind it.

Left: The smithy's interior walls were removed and Jim supported the beams with steel girders.

Opposite: *Stone Forest's* old farmhouse doorway now opens onto a mirrored alcove that delights and surprises.

Above: A pair of *Menshen* door gods protects this house and its red gate. New Year's couplets frame the gate with images of carp, a rebus for abundance. In the narrow alleyway to the right, an electricity meter has been tacked onto the wall. The meter is never read — it runs only on pre-paid cards.

Following pages: The great room of *Mumanyu* is a glass pavilion anchored by a massive brick core holding the fireplaces, flues and utilities.

Speaking the Vernacular

Frames

Of all the components of a traditional Chinese farmhouse's vernacular construction, the frame is the indisputable star. According to Ronald Knapp, author of *Chinese Houses*, one can still run across rural carpenters who learned their framing technique through poetry — via a series of mnemonic devices passed down in cadences that reflect the balance and proportion of a *tailiang*, or post-and-beam frame.

Only a skilled carpenter can piece together and set standing this skeleton of a house. In an old structure, the beams will have been the product of lavish attention, the single most expensive element of the home. Since beams had to shoulder the heavy tiled roof, they were often sourced from distant old-growth forests. Ideally, the masonry walls installed below would be curtain walls, stabilizing and hugging the posts, like stone muscle to wooden bone.

Historical craftsmen and residents paid almost as much attention to the spiritual well-being of the frame as to its technical construction. Knapp notes that a house's frame is vulnerable to omens of happiness or their opposite. Tie a red cloth emblazoned with the wrong string of words around the ridgepole, or forget to playfully wrap the pole with a pair of pants, and it might not rise. Banquets serving as elaborate expressions of gratitude to the builders and firecracker celebrations so potent as to scare off whatever sinister force has been released by the breaking of ground both preceded each roof raising.

Say a family skimps on the festive dinner, shortchanges the builders, or belittles their work; a hostile carpenter might tuck the shards of a broken rice bowl and a single chopstick into the doorframe, bringing unspeakable hardship on the household's sons and grandsons. On the other hand, a well-fed carpenter might lay a cassia leaf on the top of a column where it joins the beam, inviting luck into the home and even a happiness or two.

"It was the first day I could see the house in my mind's eye," recalls Julie Upton-Wang, a Schoolhouse partner, of the roof raising ceremony for her own house in Mutianyu, which Jim designed. "The head of the woodworking team hammered in the final big log for the ridge. The team strung firecrackers all along the ridgepole. They poured out a bottle of *baijiu*, white lightning, and lit the firecrackers to scare all the demons from inside the house. That way, when you put on the roof, there's nothing but good *feng shui*, good aura, inside. I remember it was a beautiful winter day, the sky a crystalline blue. It's pride. They take pride in their work."

Opposite: In *Heart's Repose*, Jim converted the kitchen of the peasant dwelling into a study. The space features original beams and *torchis*, blackened on one side by decades of cooking smoke. A new fireplace with concealed chimney allows for both coziness and uninterrupted views from the window above the mantle. Door frames that once led to other rooms now divide the study into bays, remaining as screens that support the beams above.

Following pages: Morning radiance at a dusty work site in Tianxianyu. The bones of this house — the window lattices minus their paper, a plank door, rafters supported by frames, which in turn are supported by narrow doorways — will be transformed into shelter for bedrooms. Across the courtyard, a newly constructed great room for living and dining will open its windows wide to the Great Wall.

The craftsmen Jim works with know their simple joinery, and one of Jim's first moves is almost always to expose a house's existing beams, right down to the mortise and tenon. Primarily, Jim loves the quality of spaciousness overhead and has, in his own home, painted the rafters black and the beams white as a further delineation of their sculptural quality. A house is best known by a look at its bones. Is the beam of the largest eastern *jian*, the biggest bay and original living space, wide enough — being barely huggable — to support the house without a masonry wall beneath it? If it is, Jim sometimes opens the original three or five rooms into a series of interconnected, airy living spaces. Perhaps there the beams are then cleaned and waxed, while in the kitchen, they are left a rich tarnished black. In any case, they are nearly always uplit by concealed rows of LEDs. The resulting interplay of space and form in relation to light draws the eye up again and again. The whole frame and headroom of the house takes on the appearance of a chandelier.

Above: The *kang* in a village home. Thick paper stretched across bamboo frames encloses the space for efficient heating while warm smoke from the kitchen wok is piped out below the *kang*, ingeniously reusing the heat generated by everyday life.

Opposite: Jim encased the original posts in stronger brick columns and extended the rooflines of this farmhouse with glass and steel, providing a dramatic but enclosed prospect of the garden beyond. As in many of his designs, Jim also uncovered the structural beams overhead. These were washed, hand polished and lighted. In this home a modest, even cramped space has been generously opened.

Following pages: Home of Schoolhouse partners Julie Upton-Wang and Peiming Wang. Jim designed asymmetrical rooflines, which nestle under the ancient, protected crown pine that defines the site. The old farmhouse peeks out at left.

Opposite: One of two master bedrooms in *Mumanyu*. Jim supported the frame with a steel I-beam to permit the removal of the masonry wall below. He also opened gaps between the frame's posts and beams, lending the suite a sense of spacious connection. He enhanced the vernacular feel by leaving the original roof exposed and untouched. It was made of light scrap and bark on which mud and straw were placed.

Above left: The lovely curve of these beams is actually a mark of their economy. Even so, the master builder responsible for *Big Rock House* judged them strong enough to stay. Jim accented their sculptural quality with a framed ceiling of white gypsum board. Bright, modern additions surround the old house with light.

Above right: Soft white linens spill onto a slate floor sourced from the roof of an old farmhouse in a *Stone Forest* bedroom. The same slate paves the entire house, including the new *kang*. Jim warmed the rubble masonry wall with a mortar of concrete mixed with mud.

Where he can, Jim often maintains the opening between the queen posts and the beams so that even separate rooms might be joined by a little trapezoidal liberation of space into space. Where such openness is not advisable, Jim has glass fitted into the frames formed by the intersection of post and beam. These small windows ensure the quiet of an office or bedroom without impeding the connection of spaces. A casual observer might spend minutes inspecting the ceiling from different angles, waiting for a shifting view of rafters and purlins to reveal whether the gaze passes through or doubles back on itself. As with the continued practice of the ridgepole ceremony — Jim's approach to the design of frames — this subtle inclusion of reflection carries an interpreted echo of the old ways. In the modern gesture of opening and connecting spaces is a smuggled whisper of a family's will to protect and preserve itself, to turn back the intrusive with a mirror-like reflection overhead.

Right: At *Ironstone*, Jim had the roof of the new building constructed with traditional rafters and modern steel beams. He accented the lofty space with a custom chandelier of copper, art glass and brass.

Opposite: *Red Door's* kitchen, where rubble masonry walls converge with a dividing wall of gray brick under the frame, leaving the entire space open to the roof. The frame has been reinforced with steel, a confluence of old and new.

Above: With a skylight cut through it, the huge roof seems to float above *Red Door's* living room. Installing the skylight required massive reinforcement, which is echoed by the solidity of the hearth at the center of the home. The double fireplace screens a *kang* across the entire end of the room, where the family curls up to watch movies and enjoy the fire.

Above: Structure at play in *Red Door*. Jim preserved the wood posts along with their lime wash, though he added steel supports to carry the heavy tile roof. Above the old purlin, a row of cathedral glass tints incoming light.

Opposite: This fireplace in the home of a French couple began with granite slabs. Jim cut a long window under the eaves, breaking tradition and opening the space to north light and a surprise view.

Right: Even close observers overlook the mirror Jim fitted above the fireplace at *Ironstone* to keep the room's monolithic anchor from closing down the space. This hearth, designed in conversation with the clients, features intricate panels that depict biblical scenes. Jim framed these in granite, affixing the panels with copper and brass shims. Custom light fixtures set off the carvings.

Below: Perched above Beigou Village, the glass house at *Eagle's Rest* adjoins the vernacular farmhouse by way of a breezeway accented with cathedral glass.

Opposite bottom: The glass and steel living room pavilion in *Eagle's Rest* is starkly juxtaposed not only with the bedroom wing but also with adjacent homes, seen here from *Mumanyu's* garden. The designs ensure both views and mutual privacy.

Following pages: At *Stone Forest*, Jim revitalized a traditional three-bay farmhouse within a graceful new build. The continuity of the neighbor's home, visible over the roof at about chimney height, affirms the attention he paid to integrating this home into its village.

Roofs

Traditional architectural vernacular in Northern China has it that a strong house needs a heavy roof — the heavier the better. The more closely scaled and efficiently wate-shedding the tiles, the higher the pitch and arch of the *yinshanding*, "firm mountain" of the roofline. This increases the weight bearing down on the columns, pressing them into their packed earth and stone foundation, steadying the house.

In modern China, the roofline is an important indicator of adherence to an inherited aesthetic. Traditional materials are still widely available: the unglazed tiles handmade in the shape of extended U's; the *jiwen* ridge mouths, terrifying mythical beasts of glazed tile ready to swallow stray sparks; the *wadang* end tiles, water-shedding anchors against the glacial creep of the tiles towards the eaves. But tastes change, and in regions where there is ample space and aggregate, the concrete box has somewhat surpassed the stone and tile temple as the vernacular of the hour — starkly flat roofs, often with decorative fake brick or reflective tile siding.

For Jim, the question is not whether to keep a roofline, but how to bring new and old together in an interesting and respectful way. "When I'm keeping an old building, it's often very hard to connect to," he admits. "This is something I've paid a lot of attention to. If you look at traditional Chinese architecture, from the Forbidden City all the way down, the rooflines don't go together very well, in my opinion. They're clunky. You have to walk outside to get to the kitchen. Just because it was done that way in the past is no reason to slavishly copy what really doesn't work. Designers have a responsibility to improve on old ways, to challenge themselves creatively."

This concern with connection, continuity and even intentional disjunction has led Jim to connect under the eaves, preserving the roofline by making the exterior into the interior. This can be seen in the glass corridor of his first commission, from a French couple, and in several other homes, including *Big Rock House* and *Persimmon Court*.

At *Stone Forest*, Jim extended the roof into a long, low-sweeping cascade of tiles. This deceptively simple maneuver required a rebuild of the whole roof, including high-tech waterproofing to allow for the use of the traditional unglazed tiles on a gentler slope. Inside, new rafters connect gracefully to the original eaves and the space flows down to form a library and lounge dug into the courtyard. This nook, bathed in sunlight year round, faces the farmhouse's now interior latticed facade and exposed stone foundation. Standing on the elevated terrace in *Stone Forest's* courtyard, the sweep of this roof carries the eye up to a panoramic view of the Great Wall.

In contrast to this graduated approach, in the master bedroom at *Red Door*, Jim broke the roofline on the north side of the ridge, introducing a slightly lower tier, which he roofed in glass for a view of the Great Wall. He bridged the new vertical gap with a clerestory of colored art glass. On sunny days the light filters through and casts tinted patterns on the floor. From outside, this treatment of the roofline resulted in the jaunty asymmetry of a long-haired girl's side part. Yet the change is also subtle enough that the house's roof still belongs in this place.

Opposite: *Stone Forest's* new corridor showcases the original hut's latticed exterior as well as its stone foundations. Jim designed hand-chiseled stepping-stones leading to the farmhouse's door. The space flows under the eaves to the right, forming a reading retreat warmed by a skylight.

Below: Set in a nook with windows on three sides, *Stone Forest's kang* faces the home's fireplace and also offers year-round views of the Great Wall. The low table is a traditional feature of *kang* living — lounging, dining and sleeping.

Top: The asymmetrical roofline of the new master suite at *Red Door* speaks to the original peasant dwelling, now turned into one great room. Skylights on the suite's lower roof allow for spectacular views of the Great Wall from the bed.

Above: Dramatic skylights, along with an assortment of windows large and small, provide kaleidoscopic views from *Mumanyu's* kitchen and dining room. The whole interior shifts with the changing light and seasons.

Opposite: The skylight in the addition to the right of *Mumanyu's* farmhouse fills the master shower with sun throughout the year. The other roof opening provides light to the added living room, which seems to flow through the original structure in a river of glass and steel.

Below: Jim punctuated the high, sloping roofline of *Mumanyu's* living room with a well-placed skylight, opening to a view of the Great Wall, while also creating the exciting illusion of not a single neighboring home.

Opposite: *Hillside Haven's* dining room is open to nature. The table sits by the stone wall of an original *er-fang*, now one of the home's two bedrooms. Above the peaked roofline of the *er-fang* is a wall of glass composing the south facade of the new building. That building was constructed on the site of the original farmhouse, long ago dismantled, leaving only its smaller outbuildings, the *er-fang*, to be preserved in the new home.

Following pages: In this getaway for a movie director, angular steel roofs make space for unusual clerestories. White painted concrete floors serve as the simple anchor for an elegant, contemporary living space.

"There's a crown pine behind my house that's very important to the village," says Julie. "It's the oldest or second-oldest tree in the area, and our house is said to have excellent *feng shui* because of its proximity. Jim put a lot of attention into carrying the slope of the pine branches into the roof. It was lovely to watch that process."

Though his respect for rooflines dovetails with his attention to a house's vital relationship to its surroundings, Jim occasionally breaks his own rules. In the home he built in Beigou for a movie director, Jim dealt with low walls and ceilings by removing the existing roof altogether.

"I kept all of the original facade, all the original framing," he explains, "and then I did four walls of windows up above and put a new roof on it. This steel roof is on a single plane, not parallel to the earth — one corner is much higher than the others. The mold is broken and the beams become isolated, like they're floating; they become literal sculpture and the roof just floats away."

Walls

"China's is a wall-building culture," Jim explains. "If it's yours — your home or your China — you put a wall around it to keep your people in and everyone else out. Peasant houses out here aren't really traditional courtyard houses in the sense of a *siheyuan*, the way they are in Beijing where three or four long buildings frame a central garden. The peasants here were just too poor. They had everything in one little row house. But now, as soon as they get enough money, they put up walls. High walls. Heavy gates."

Jim's architectural practice began with and continues to center on the home, so what is privately within never fails to amaze and compel him. When he builds a house in the villages he too puts up walls. These walls serve to link his new and old dwellings into the structural fabric of the working village around them, while creating ample room for play within.

"If you have a wall outside, then the house can be transparent," Jim says. "People want to feel safe, sheltered, but they also want to feel connected to nature, so the challenge is to balance the two."

At *Heart's Repose*, a stunning house for a Danish family, which also happens to sit on Mutianyu's only and sometimes busy road, Jim has built a three-sided glass structure, which houses a shower under a glass roof. This rain pavilion is entirely open to the outdoors, but in a twist on traditional Chinese nested spaces, the surrounding private garden is walled even within the house's private central courtyard. At this house, as in many, Jim has brought the vertiginous awe of Great Wall views into a maximally private space.

Right: The back entrance of a Mutianyu residence designed with a nod to the local vernacular courtyard doorways. Jim made harmony of a variety of masonry: recycled bricks cobbled into the drive, fieldstone walls with white mortar, and red brick caps. His custom light fixtures, 40 in all, are of copper and brass. Traditional gate signs mark the doors with wishes for happiness in the New Year.

Opposite: The Great Wall at Mutianyu forms the constructed spine of some of the oldest exposed stone on the face of the earth.

"When you're dealing in walls you're also dealing in windows," Jim says. "For example, if you're sitting propped up in bed and looking out my bedroom window, you don't see our courtyard wall, the road, or the car; all you see are mountains and sky. To have that felt experience of wide expanse, of freedom, there also has to be an implicit sense of safety and enclosure."

This sense of protective enclosure, almost of refuge, becomes most vulnerable where the courtyard wall breaks, namely at the entryway. Chinese architecture is preoccupied with this issue and has frequently solved it with an elegant spirit wall, a decorative masonry screen or freestanding short wall, which interrupts the view from an open gate into the private courtyard. This little wall protects against all entrances immaterial — from an overly curious eye to an evil one. In Jim's design, the spirit wall also plays an important role in the curating of views and the visitor's experience of meeting a house.

"Most of my houses have something like a spirit wall, but not always in the traditional sense," Jim reflects. "You take *Ironstone* — my client wanted a dramatic entrance to the house so I renovated a pre-existing agricultural shack in the lower lawn to act like a kind of screen. It's a beautiful stone structure; all we had to do was repair it. When you come through the gate you're confronted with the dry stone wall of the shack. You can't see the house at all. So you get that element of surprise, the juxtaposition between what is small, and old and beautiful, and what is bigger and newer and also lovely — the house itself."

Opposite: The *Heart's Repose* master bathroom can offer unobstructed Great Wall views because it adjoins a separate and very private courtyard used by the owner as a refuge to practice yoga. The shower projects into the courtyard and its wooden lattices reveal while protecting.

Above: The *Persimmon Court* master bedroom was created from the existing farmhouse.

Following pages: Jim adapted this residence from an abandoned seven-bay warehouse. Moving away from the vernacular treatment of load-bearing walls, Jim opened the space by cutting three windows into the thick east wall. This approach is mirrored by a glass gable in the attached kitchen and dining pavilion. Jim's interest in transparency, color and light has also found its way to the art glass lighting he designed to flank the entryway.

Above: In the construction of *Ironstone's* main gate, local granite blocks were hand-chiseled on site while the lintel was specially quarried and lowered into place by a crane. The massive doors were fabricated from local walnut and their copper and brass fixtures fashioned to Jim's design by an area craftsman. During the year-long construction of *Ironstone*, many of these craftspeople became not just neighbors, but friends of the homeowners.

Opposite: A found sculpture at *Stone Forest* defines and protects the home's entryway, which curves to the left.

In fact, a visitor to *Ironstone* transitions through not one but two interconnected points of entry marking a progression of increasingly private spaces, the first at the stone shack, and the second after a winding path and stairs which lead to the home's intimate outdoor living room.

"*Ironstone* has a lower and an upper garden and I designed that second space as a more literal extension of the house," explains Jim. "To protect it, we installed a very traditional spirit wall. It was drawn from the local contractor's pattern book for spirit walls, built of brick and plastered. The bricks were handcarved to cantilever out and support gold glazed tiles made at the factory that is now the boutique hotel I designed, the Brickyard."

Jim's traditional treatment of this screen exhibits the same craft and sense of place that informed his use of the shed. Jim chose his colors and materials with care and an eye for local workmanship and components. He designed the paths to the outdoor living spaces that wind near and around the second spirit wall, allowing visitors and residents alike a close-up view of its tile roof.

Top: A neighbor's dry-stone shed, adjacent to *Eagle's Rest*, preserved and integrated into the home's courtyard wall.

Above: The entryway to *Big Rock House* winds up stony stairs to a boulder guarding the doorway and a wild garden in counterpoint to the modern lines of the new home.

Right: An existing agricultural shed was rebuilt with salvaged lattice and doors at the entryway of *Ironstone*. The dry stone construction wall on the left is a visitor's first view upon entering the property, a testament both to craft and to Jim's creative engagement with the vernacular of spirit walls. Jim installed a rope of LEDs, concealed behind a gray line of angle steel, to wash the wall in light during the evening.

Previous pages: After entering the lower courtyard at *Ironstone*, the door to the main house is protected by another *ying bei*, or spirit wall, at the top of the steps where there is an outdoor living room and another garden. The glazed yellow tiles were made right in Beigou village. One of the old houses incorporated in *Ironstone* is to the left of the spirit wall and has been opened up with west-facing windows.

Right: *Big Rock House's* eponymous *in situ* boulder forms the hearth and anchor point of the living room. Juxtaposed angular steps, capped in native white granite, lead into the living space. Glass ceilings and high windows provide an ever-changing panorama of the Great Wall in all its moods and lights. The free-standing fireplace of painted steel and hammered copper was handmade by local craftspeople.

Left: Named for the lucky hue of its entrance gate, *Red Door* stands open, welcoming passersby to take note of the blue and white cloud tiles commissioned as a screen. After entering, visitors turn up stairs leading to a surprise inner courtyard. The native ivy spanning the courtyard wall is a hardy, small-leafed variety that flares purple and red for a few days each fall.

Right: Part of the client's collection of Chinese antiques, these huge wooden doors seal off the underground opening to the original farmhouse wing of *Ironstone*. During the rainy season, the exposed foundations on the left turn into a spring, which flows harmlessly into a sump.

Following pages: *Ironstone's* underground cigar and wine tasting room adjoins the wine cellar. Jim accented the rough stone walls with finely carpentered walnut, seen here in the fireplace surround, the frames of the alcove lighting and the ceiling lattice. Hand-cut granite squares on the fireplace complete the architectural decoration.

Facades

Houses in China are built facing south. Their eastern and western flanks and thick northern backs are typically windowless so as to shelter residents from biting winds and flurries of snow. It is the southern facade that gives a farmhouse its character, like eyes open to the warming sun, to neighboring homes, the surrounding landscape, as well as to the elements.

Where it seems right to do so, Jim restores and preserves the traditional wood-latticed exterior of an original building. In some cases, as in the house Jim designed for his mother, he changes nothing at all. At *Grandma's Place*, the original paint — a robin's egg blue — chips from the delicate latticework. Normally, such a lattice opens all along a house's upper half and, in winter, only a coating of thick paper would separate kitchen and *kang* from the snowy yard. As winter gave way to spring and summer, the paper would wear thin and fray, allowing the light and warmth that filled the valley to flood into the home as well.

Today, designing homes with modern heating, Jim still makes use of the blurring of indoor and outdoor space. In a house in Tianxianyu aptly named *Heart's Desire*, which may offer the finest vistas of a series of homes graced by stunning views, the window lattices have been left unglazed to create a small open foyer in the house's central bay, which abuts two refurbished bedrooms. In the sleeping quarters, the new windows have been framed and hung within the lattice, creating a smooth and unencumbered envelope of the traditional around the modern.

Right: Traditional latticework and cobbled floors have found their way into Jim's aesthetic, while the rhythms and innovations of the surrounding villages have informed his commitment to sustainability. Beneath this kitchen's built-in wok, plant refuse is recycled as cooking fuel.

Opposite: A view into one of the bedrooms at either side of *Heart's Desire's* semi-outdoor foyer, which was created from the kitchen of the farmhouse. The unglazed lattice, plank doors, torchis and smoke-blackened rafters are all original. The bedrooms have exterior-grade doors to protect from the elements.

"An old house is like putty," muses Jim, "something to play with, a malleable starting point. I'm not particularly interested in preservation *per se*. To take an old house and preserve its exterior and overall feel while making it run like a 21st-century space is a little more interesting, but still not quite to my taste."

Jim's taste runs towards what he identifies as living architecture. For a house to live, it must surprise, even challenge, its occupants. To Jim's mind, if there is a structural conversation between elements new and old, if a trace of the maker's hand survives honored and affirmed by new additions, then a house has a pulse and so much the better for the people who live inside and alongside it.

"For me it's a sense of history," Jim clarifies. "I've never been keen on building a new house that pretends to be an old one. I'm also not interested in adding onto an old house so you can't tell what's old and what's new. I like juxtaposition and contrast."

Even at *Heart's Desire*, where Jim was so attentive to the preservation of the original facade, the old house faces a contemporary independent structure containing the open-plan kitchen and living room. This new build's scaled-up *kang* has a modern heating element that abuts a wood stove. A story-and-a-half wall of glazed tile mosaic rises behind the stove. Across from the *kang*, a glass wall opens to the view of the Yanshan Mountains — dizzyingly close and steep, knuckled by white granite that is said to be some of the oldest exposed stone on Earth.

In Jim's own house, the disjunction between old and new is less severe, although he has designed an asymmetrical series of additions, which give the home a sense of organic growth. Jim unified this juxtaposition of heights, of renovated and preserved facades, with a thin white thread. This outdoor chair rail stitches the house together over its two wings, multiple add-ons and terraced courtyards.

Opposite: The site mandated a low ceiling for this cozy dining room, so Jim designed a cracked ice-pattern lattice under the lighting and mechanics, giving a sense of endless open sky above. The north window offers an intimate view of the home's incorporated farmhouse. The *teppanyaki* table was a requirement of the owners and Jim devised the hand-crafted walnut surround to make an inviting focal point around which friends and family gather. The lattice above was handmade from pine and left unfinished to age gracefully like the rafters of a traditional home.

Bottom left: Steel tubing with recessed LED lighting frames this free-standing glass pavilion and invites comparison to the preserved facade of one of Mutianyu's oldest homes, which is now the master suite of *Pavilion*. This juxtaposition of old and new is at the heart of Jim's aesthetic.

Bottom right: Only the facade remains of this farmhouse now connected by an asymmetrical glass roof to the home's new building. As Jim says, "Harmony is not the only way to marry new and old."

Following pages: Inside the original facade, Jim constructed a glass curtain wall for privacy, light and energy efficiency. While preserving the facade, he made the old building itself a modern synthesis. Instead of hiding the farmhouse's redeployment to a new use, it is celebrated.

Courtyards

The *yuan*, or courtyard, is a traditional Chinese house's inside-out heart, the essential 3,000-year-old core around which the *siheyuan*, the Beijing residential enclosure known as a courtyard house, breathes and lives. Even outside Beijing, no house is a Chinese house without a certain amount of buffer space, both outdoors and private, surrounded yet open to the light and weather.

"I haven't built any houses that are traditional Beijing courtyards. People do housing developments out here and doctor them up like fake *siheyuans*. To my mind it's ugly. You take something that was never here and plop it down. Also they tend to be glitzy. It's not to my taste but I'm a snob," Jim laughs, "I'm a total snob."

Jim begins with village farmhouses, single row dwellings often lacking even a wall to mark the edge of the property. Because of this, his treatment of the *yuan* is largely additive and occasionally unorthodox. In some cases he does develop something like the traditional courtyard, adding another wing to an old house and rounding out a defined central space. More often, Jim retains the long connecting yards common throughout the village, incorporating this external zone into the home's interior with a glass corridor or continuous paving indoors and out.

Right: At Hillside Haven only the *er-fang*, the "ear-rooms" or small detached structures, of the original farmhouse remained. Jim built a new two-story structure of glass, brick and steel on the old footprint. He addressed issues of connecting rooflines with a central glass entryway of the same scale as the flanking *er-fang*.

Opposite: Where does the old stop and the new begin? In this Mutianyu residence only the ridgeline seen at the top is original; everything else was added. Here, respect for the old house is revealed inside.

Right: Why is *Heart's Repose* so inviting? In Jim's words, "Here, the new building is raised on a podium and is the same lateral dimensions as the original farmhouse. Raising it opens views which would otherwise be obstructed. Putting the main building to the south also breaks with convention. The connecting hallway has light wells at each end and its higher roof allows for clerestory windows in the two bedrooms behind the hall. Entry steps on the left are stone blocks hand-chiseled on site, as are the curbstones. Paving is re-used brick scraps. The lattices made of pine and walnut echo the original home, tying the composition together."

Previous pages: The siting of this rude stone farmhouse was perfect, surrounded by row upon row of hills and mountains receding forever. In Chinese this panorama is called *shanluan* and the local people lived with it always. The long glass hallway here reveals the untouched facade, while transforming the vernacular into something elegant and modern.

Left: This long, low hallway tucked into the hillside connects two farmhouses combined into one home, creating a courtyard for outdoor living as well as a dramatic display space for collections.

Below: The vernacular of a high courtyard wall, overflowing with vines and stacked above two retaining walls, allows this farmhouse the exterior privacy for a traditional facade of sunny windows.

In the narrow alley of 'downtown' Mutianyu at *Pavilion*, Jim has filled the courtyard with a contemporary steel building walled on three sides by glass and featuring a large skylight. Inside the structure, a sunken fireplace is surrounded by a rising amphitheater of rectangular white granite steps. The space is reminiscent of an outdoor campfire, or a sort of theater for the sleek firebox. Across from the fireplace, a glossy kitchenette is backed by a wall of polished black granite that catches reflections of the nearby Great Wall. Across the outdoor courtyard stands the village's oldest house. Entirely preserved on the outside, the interior space is a cozy and simple master bedroom separated from its open-plan bathroom by a half wall. Though separated by function, the bays remain visually one space as in the great room at *Red Door*. A small window has been cut into the thick north wall of the *Pavilion's* master bedroom, offering a view up the mountainside and a subtle reminder of the home's synthesis of old and new.

The secret garden, a patio with adjoining vegetable cellar, is carved into the hill and supported by rough stone retaining walls. Tucked behind *Pavilion's* original structure, the patio is both a retreat into the wilds of the rough hillside and a private viewing platform. The view looks out across the village, row upon row of unglazed tiles as they rise up to the *Zheng Guan Tai*, the highly distinctive three-tower gate that defines the central portion of the Mutianyu Great Wall.

Above: The *Pavilion's* secret terrace is wedged on the mountainside behind the home. The stone walls are original and the doorway leads to a cave-like root cellar where fruits and vegetables were stored year-round at constant temperature. A medley of broken brick paving used to create the terrace offers year-round color.

Right: This glass and steel living room opens to the garden and panoramic views beyond neighboring village houses. The *Pavilion's* core is a simple hearth surrounded by granite steps that continue outside.

Memory and Innovation: Building One Home

Opposite: Everything extraneous stripped away, the transformation of a farmhouse into a new home marrying traditional and modern is about to begin.

Above left: Looking west from the master bedroom through the new hallway inside the original facade. There are two bedrooms and a shared bath off the hallway, which then turns left, becoming a newly built corridor to the great room across the courtyard. These rooms have windows onto the hallway but are also lit with skylights and nontraditional windows cut through the farmhouse's massive north wall. A sliding door frame has been mounted on the left so that the narrow hallway isn't obstructed when one uses the original doorway to the outside.

Above right: The two-bay *kang* room on the east end of the farmhouse becomes the master bedroom. A doorway to an added-on bathroom is cut in the end wall. Jim also installed a hanging fireplace that opens onto and warms both spaces. Gray brick provides support to the wall and post. The rubble walls have been highlighted with a custom blend of mud and concrete. The native slate floor has been laid but is obscured and intentionally protected by construction dust until the final cleaning. These process pictures were all taken on the same day, late in the building project.

Opposite top: The outlines of what will become a courtyard are now evident — old farmhouse, connecting corridor at the far end and high great room facing north to the Great Wall. The roof tiles of the old farmhouse were removed, insulation and waterproofing added, and then reinstalled. Plantings were started before the home was complete in order not to miss a season of growth.

Opposite bottom left: A view into the great room from the breezeway and main entry. The low flat ceiling allows for a rooftop terrace accessed by an exterior staircase. On the left will be the utility/laundry room, a closet, and a lavatory. Up two steps and to the left, but still under the flat ceiling, is the open kitchen. The high-ceilinged great room invites beyond.

Opposite bottom middle: Inside the connecting corridor. Thermal-paned windows face a lattice patterned to match that of the original farmhouse. On the right the existing garden wall has been raised, reinforced with steel posts and insulated on the other side. Jim will install recessed LED lights to wash the wall. The ceiling will be painted black and offset with an unfinished pine lattice. At the far end of the corridor is a small high window bringing light into the library corner of the great room and offering glimpses of sky as one walks through the corridor.

Opposite bottom right: Massive beams, set onto reinforced concrete columns clad with gray brick, support the middle of the seemingly traditional roof, which actually includes open gables on both ends. The steel tubes intercrossing the beams are not structural; they will hold LED down spots as well as uplights toward the warm wood of the ceiling. The north windows have already been installed with lower sliding panes for ventilation and huge panels above, creating the views that inspired the design. The horizontal strip of pine brings the richness of wood to a human level while disguising the steel tubes bracing the columns. A built-in window seat conceals storage and runs the length of the window wall.

Top left: There is a story behind this window's inclusion in the home, says Jim. "I love little windows and this house already had several designed into it but in reviewing the early plans with my friend Zhong Wenkai, he suggested that a tall and narrow window here would be a modern touch and provide surprise light and views. Design of even so simple a thing as a house can be collaborative and can benefit from suggestions and insights. I have had so much help and encouragement and often my own ideas blend into borrowings, really downright theft, I guess."

Above: Full circle — the great room from the west end where the connecting corridor joins the library nook, two steps down and tucked under a low ceiling. Air conditioning is hidden above, out of view of the open gable. The raised hearth contains space for storing logs. Clerestory windows on the south wall welcome light without sacrificing privacy from the adjacent lane.

Left: Fog shrouds the mountains to the west as dusk settles over Tianxianyu's newest home.

Opposite bottom: The finished great room faces north for a view of the old farmhouse facade with the mountains above.

Bottom: Orient yourself to this home, built for a French family, with the drawings printed in the back endpapers of this book.

The Garden Factory

The Great Wall has long stood as a kind of inheritance, a physical structure endowed with memory and collective significance. Is it possible to extend that reverence not just to a humble farmhouse, but even further to a factory building or a fragment of traditional glazed tile? Not only is it possible, concludes architect Wenkai Zhong, Jim's friend and collaborator, but this frame of mind is as central to Jim's commercial work as it is to his residential designs. It is that very feeling of home, of inhabiting structures built into an ongoing story, that draws visitors to the Brickyard Eco-Retreat.

The oldest structures at the Brickyard frame a central courtyard. Jim composed the property so that the new buildings angle away from the center without the regimented feeling of a perpendicular intersection. The original buildings — the line of nine kilns once used to fire glazed tiles, the workers' dormitory, the tile showroom — were preserved, allowing function and playfulness to shape their new design.

Jim converted the kilns into unique public spaces, including offices, washrooms and a video lounge. The original chimneys, preserved as skylights, form unexpected little windows. Jim also retained the walls' highly textured refractory surface, deciding it was an integral part of the feeling of the repurposed spaces.

"You can see this layer of mud applied to the brick, which is crumbling away," notes Zhong. "Most people wouldn't think to preserve something like that, but it becomes part of a story — almost a mural or relief. Those walls went through fire."

Opposite: The operating glazed tile factory did not have a blade of glass and was filled with rubbish, inventory and huge piles of wood for firing tiles when Liang spotted the temple roof of the plant office and the Sleeping Buddha protecting it. She knew that this decrepit and polluting artifact of misguided development could be transformed into the oasis it is today.

Left: Jim placed the water tower needed to ensure the retreat's constant supply atop the kiln, a perfect location for signs using the logo he had designed for the Brickyard.

At his hotel, as in the homes he designs, Jim's aesthetic is as guided by function, by the needs of those who will use the spaces, as it is by the memory of local materials and buildings. In the kiln rooms, he specially designed ceilings of tempered glass and steel, which not only serve to light the rooms with integrated LEDs but also to reflect that light back into the space while protecting occupants from the fragments, which occasionally crumble from the original vaulted ceiling.

Jim replaced the rotted out rafters of the factory dormitory and re-laid the traditional tiles, adding a blue glazed tile ridge to underline the distant views. He repurposed the rooms below as meeting spaces. With the only finished interior walls at the Brickyard painted in a bright yellow, this open and energizing work space stands in contrast to the relaxed warmth and texture that characterizes the rest of the retreat.

At the center of the Brickyard, temple-grade glazed tiles produced on site crown the Lodge. Jim wholly preserved the elaborate gold, green and turquoise roof as the unmistakable focal point of the central courtyard. From here, the Brickyard's newly built rooms stretch out in rows along a series of terraces on the property's southwestern flank.

Right: A dirt track once led to the factory, which lacked a wall or even a fence around it. Jim created a road and parking area, separated from the hotel's entry courtyard by this wall.

Opposite: This massive stone, exposed on both sides, was emplaced first and each brick cut to fit its contours as the new wall rose track by track around it.

"I didn't want to design an ordinary hotel," Jim explains. "I wanted something like a garden factory, a walk-in motel. That, in conversation with a kept industrial feeling. I didn't try to replicate the tile roofs all over the property, because that's not how people generally build factories or peasant homes in Northern China. Corrugated steel. Grey, industrial, even utilitarian. How is it possible for that to be beautiful? It comes from simplicity, from the structures' clean lines which are then interrupted by encroaching, often flowering, growth."

Jim terraced the land to ensure that every one of the Brickyard's 25 guest rooms features views of the Great Wall. The four banks of rooms are separated by winding paths, carp ponds and semi-private courtyards. Working with a relatively confined color palette, Jim softened a built environment of brick, slate and glass with planted species long cultivated by villagers for food production and ornamentation. In juxtaposition to the original structures, the newly built rooms' red brick and asymmetrical steel roofs flare out to story-and-a-half window walls. The interiors are luxuriously simple: brick walls, floors of dark native slate. The first three rows of queen rooms are low at the door and rise towards the window wall.

Zhong is particularly taken with these north-facing spaces, which are highly unusual in an area where *feng shui* has long dictated that buildings open to the south. "I think for those who have lived so long in this place, the Wall has entered their subconscious. They don't need to see it. They know it is there. In a hotel, the view is a great advantage and the siting of the Brickyard rooms creates views of the Great Wall from every corner. In the final row, which is actually at a lower elevation than the one preceding it, the rooms are entered through a private garden, which creates enough space for views of the Wall over the nearby roofs."

Opposite: The Lodge's stunning roof has pride of place in Jim's design. Gray steel roofs on all the new buildings provide understated company to the decorative use of glazed tiles in a spectrum of colors.

Above: The Brickyard Lodge and its temple-grade tiled roof are protected by traditional *wenshou*, the flamboyant Chinese equivalent of the gargoyle. A phoenix-riding godling is followed by four mythical beasts of ascending size and complexity.

Above: Like Mutianyu and many other mountain villages in Bohai Township, Beigou flows south, down from a ravine in the Yanshan Mountains. The Brickyard occupies part of the desirable flat land. Its courtyards, gardens, and guest rooms all share this view of the mountains and Great Wall. The layout can be seen in the as-built plans for the property, which are reproduced in the front endpapers of this book.

Opposite: "This arched arcade buttresses the unsound structure of the old kiln," says Jim. "It also echoes the barrel vaults forming the kiln chambers, as well as those in the Great Wall guard towers." Jim complemented the design with three little openings at the far end to draw in visitors.

Left: The kiln building is fronted by an entry arcade forming the south edge of the Brickyard's main courtyard. Nine little windows have been placed in the screen at the end of the courtyard that protects the outdoor room adjacent to the Lodge and blocks the view to the second courtyard beyond. After the screen was completed, Jim added the bit of stone wall in relief as decoration.

"Even the names of the rooms refer back to the landscape," continues Zhong, "Sleeping Buddha in honor of the nearby mountain formation, Chairman's Suite in reference to the hillside slogan which reads, 'Be Loyal to Chairman Mao.' All of this serves to situate the buildings within their context, as does the use of materials specific to the site."

"These are what I love," says Jim, hand against an entryway wall mosaic. "Kiln workers placed small stilts on these refractory bricks to lay glazed tiles on for firing. The glaze dripped down, mixing all the colors of this place: green of trees, yellow sun, blue sky, red earth. Eventually glaze and tile fragments would build up and the bricks would be torn out and replaced." When Jim acquired the property he dug up the refractory bricks, which had been used to pave the courtyard or tossed away in rubbish piles, and invited local masons to piece together custom mosaics for each of the queen rooms.

"Jim has a particular talent for finding resources like these," says Zhong. "He dug up what had been considered garbage and deployed it not just as decoration, but as a reminder of place."

The Brickyard's history as a glazed tile factory has also worked its way into myriad pathways, spirit walls and custom lighting installations mosaiced with fragments of the tiles themselves.

"Glazed tiles are an essential part of traditional Chinese architecture," notes Zhong, "but when they're placed on rooftops like they were used to, they seem distant and aloof because they signify authority and prestige. By dispersing these tiles, these pigments, into the landscape, Jim brings them down and close to us, reminding us that these colors are all part of the environment already."

Above: This unembellished nine-ton stone stands in the main courtyard, in counterpoint to the ornate Lodge roof.

Right: The hotel Activity Center, shown here, was originally the factory dormitory. A decorative line of sawn blue tiles is flush with the adjacent wall; its color is threaded throughout the property, including the Activity Center's ridge tiles and wooden lintels.

Above: This *ying bei* protects and announces the Brickyard with gold and blue hand-cut tiles. The characters *wa chang* mean tile factory. "It lines up directly with the entrance to the property," notes Jim, "but the wall is also decorative and was intended to be an irresistible photo opportunity for guests."

Right: This simple and low lean-to, a common tactic for enlarging local homes, was tacked onto the Lodge to create a lounge. Zhong Wenkai observes that fireplaces, which are not part of China's architectural tradition, become the new soul of Jim's buildings paired with the courtyards that are their China-inspired heart.

Following pages: When the factory office was turned into a lodge, the four *jian* needed to be opened into one room but the beams were not competent, nor were the masonry walls strong enough to support the structure safely. So Jim added concealed foundations and steel reinforcement, which became part of the industrial aesthetic. The wood in the bar and the shelves behind it, as well as cabinets in the Activity Center and a massive outdoor table, all came from one Beigou walnut tree that died during an especially cold winter.

"You have to be careful with how much tile you use," Jim cautions. "The tiles are meant to be a side dish, not a main. If you have too much, it will be a distraction; too little, it will be a distraction. I consciously look at each project and think how it will be used, like a movie set in which each detail matters. And though I'm a firm believer in respecting function, there's something in the human soul that wants things to be decorated."

Whole glazed tiles cap a steel arbor, a series of peaks supported by rafters not unlike a traditional Chinese roof, which flanks the western side of the spa garden north of the main courtyard.

"For me, the arbor is not just a decorative piece of landscape," says Zhong, "it can be seen as an abstract piece of architecture. I found that to be very beautiful both conceptually and physically."

In the center of the garden, next to a yoga platform and lily pond, stands a three-sided brick shelter which creates a sense of seclusion on the platform as well as respite from heat and sun. The structure's brick back faces onto the kitchen garden. Ceramic fragments form Chinese characters that read in English as: *When you drink the water, don't forget who dug the well.*

This aphorism in broken tiles embodies the qualities of remembrance, connection and appreciation that draw all kinds of people to the Brickyard. It also articulates an aspect of Jim's architectural practice that is as rooted in social relationships as it is in materiality. Local craft and materials have not only informed the Brickyard's unique architecture and design innovations, they have connected this garden factory to Jim's ongoing process of building home.

Above: Another example of structural reinforcement, here integrated with the lighting system. These meeting tables in the Activity Center are part of the Brickyard's elm furnishings designed by Jim and hand-built in a countryside factory. Two of Han Weiqiang's studies for a mural commissioned by Jim hang on the far wall.

Right: Photography stylist Ampol Paul J arranged this jumble of the Brickyard's furniture in conversation with the collection of prints from the Great Proletarian Cultural Revolution, which presides over the meeting room.

Left: Jim reinforced the barrel vault of this room, which he created from a kiln chamber, with steel. The crumbling refractory surface, a swirling mixture of clay and mud applied to brick walls, is now washed by recessed lighting. The south window, visible at center, was originally the loading door of the kiln and this room is now entered from a new opening cut through the meter-thick north wall.

Below: The craftsman Jim tasked with building this spirit wall made a slight miscalculation resulting in the left column of tiles and eyes being truncated. "There's something about imperfections like that," Zhong notes, "They make people feel comfortable by reminding them an actual human being is responsible for what is around them."

Bottom: This glazed tile sign reads *wa chang* and the fragments were hand-cut to give the characters a brushstroke-like quality.

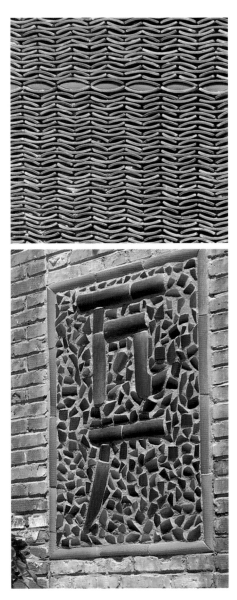

Opposite: Brickyard hotel rooms open onto semi-private courtyards; this is the first in a series. Jim punctuated industrial steel roofing with bright, south-facing skylights.

Left: The low-slung rooms in the front row of the Brickyard allow for views of the mountains and Great Wall over the roofline. A slightly lower roof on the arcade connecting the rooms conceals vents above. The rooms themselves open into massive window walls with panoramic views.

Below: The window walls of the guestrooms reflect their view and give onto private terraces.

Above: The entryway of a queen room photographed and reflected from the open-plan bathroom. Jim hired local masons to piece together these mosaics from recycled refractory bricks.

Opposite: Only the mullions remind us that this guest room is not outdoors.

Opposite: Evening in one of the retreat's contemplative guest rooms. At night the sky is filled with stars.

Above: The Sleeping Buddha room seems set in the treetops.

Left: Soaring open bath in the Chairman's Suite. Rainforest shower and soaking tub behind it. Guests luxuriate in the views.

Left: Sunlit treatment suite in the Spa, opening onto a private courtyard. Guests in the sauna, several steps up from the massage room, are surprised by views of the Wall from the interior window, top right. In the evening, two mosaic strips provide a soft glow.

Top: The Spa garden, paths paved in brick recycled from the factory sheds. From spring to fall the kitchen plot, at left, is intensely cultivated: lettuce, chives, spinach, peppers, cabbage.

Bottom: The lotus pond is at the center of the Spa garden, here overlooked by the treatment rooms.

Above: Nature offers up blue sky, scudding clouds and mountains to sunbathers in this private courtyard.

Opposite: Jim's abstract steel and tile arbor on the west side overlooks corn fields and orchards. In this spring picture, four thousand irises are blooming. In years to come the arbor will be overgrown by honeysuckle and wisteria, the tiles visible only in winter.

Building Home

"**S**ite is the beginning of making the space. What I mean by this is not just the lay of the land," Jim explains, "or even where the sun comes up. It's also the social environment and what is already built around you. These Chinese villages are home to families who have been here five hundred years, families and clans with ties to the land and affections for it, who think of themselves as its stewards."

Building in areas where a dwelling's site is as social as it is topographical, Jim begins with questions pointing toward conversation as well as juxtaposition. For regardless of how a new dwelling is constructed, designing a home in the villages means joining the flow of a conversation that started many centuries ago. How to enter? Interruption is a possibility, and under certain circumstances a fantastically modern house complements and supports the vernacular architecture surrounding it.

"To build something very evidently new, that's a different way of speaking to what's around," says Jim. "I'm not saying that's good or bad, it's a choice that depends upon the community you're in. Another way, the one I've chosen, is a middle road.

"From a Western perspective, the middle path is often looked down on intellectually — you're not this and you're not that, so you must be nothing. But here, working in these villages, I think the middle road means respecting scale and tradition but also stretching them."

This middle way has led Jim to design homes that surprise even the casual passerby, houses that emerge and recede from the tapestry of the village's built environment. From one angle, Jim's houses are indistinguishable. From another, they catch the eye and hold it, inspiring curiosity in locals and visitors alike.

With his trademark mix of bluntness and reflection, Jim observes, "When I'm designing a home, what I want to respect is not just a crummy little hut but the sense of a village and how the houses are all the same and yet each one is different. A piecemeal approach by individual owners, changing and upgrading — that's what's alive. What isn't is when a higher power comes in, kicks the peasants out and slavishly restores a museum."

In sharp contrast to large-scale displacement and unilaterally manufactured "restoration," Jim aims to integrate new dwellings, and new families, into the villages and their communities without displacing either residents or the homes they are leasing.

"The main reason I don't just tear down buildings is because of that sense of history and place," Jim explains. "It's also because of concerns with the overall carbon footprint. If you use an existing building, you've saved a lot of material and energy. The problem is, these little huts weren't the kind of grand mansions that give you wonderful spaces that typically I, or my clients, would want. How do you take something that was a poor person's home, remember that with respect, and yet turn it into something that is grand in its own way?"

From a community perspective, this work is complex. It's part of a change that began in 1986 with the opening of the Mutianyu Great Wall and it lives out in developments which could turn the village into the model of a modern rural community in China, or into a glassed-in pseudo village, or worst of all into a ghost town. "Gentrification is not necessarily a good thing," Jim qualifies, "but when the local community is on the point of dying, maybe thoughtful gentrification has an honest purpose."

Jim's upbringing across the United States introduced him to towns and cities in essence segregated by class. The rich people lived in one area, with nearby grocery stores and quality schools, while service providers commuted to work from areas that lacked the educational, health and safety services of the wealthy employing districts.

"There's a lot in the saying, 'It takes a village'," Jim notes. "It's more than just raising a good person; it's about what makes a community. How can people understand and respect each other if they don't live together? At the same time, I do think there's an inescapable truth to that line spoken by the neighbor in the poem "Mending Wall" by Robert Frost: 'Good fences make good neighbors.' No one is saying that the life of a diverse community is an easy one, or that things can't fall apart in tragic ways. Infrastructure needs to respond to the challenges of living together, to support a dynamic balance point between public and private with both well-designed communal zones and intimate retreats.

"Throughout history there have been different levels in society, some rich and some poor, but there's a basic sense of equality, really empathy, that can come from living together. That's what I hope for when I build a house for a client out here, right in the middle of a rural community. No, leasing a disused house doesn't make a village family wealthy overnight, but it does free up some of the equity they have in the land. That money, these days around USD 100,000 because the area's property values have gone up, goes directly to the household. People use it in intelligent and inventive ways: to take care of their elderly, to send kids to school, to make improvements on their own homes."

Jim's conviction that people begin to care about the same community when they start to live together comes directly from his own experience of moving to Mutianyu, getting prodded by the village mayor to contribute, and opening The Schoolhouse.

The ramifications of Jim's home building echo not just in the local economy and community but also in the broader built environment. "What is most flattering to me," Jim says, "is that now when local people in the villages have the money and are rebuilding, they take some of our ideas to make their homes more livable. A luxury of simplicity — you don't need to have a huge house."

This focus on livability over scale has much in common with Organic Architecture, a theory first put forward by Frank Lloyd Wright. With their broad attention to the dynamics of site and a house's own particular and ongoing life, the principles of Organic Architecture have inspired and informed Jim's own practice of building home from preexisting structures in a rural community. His houses locate themselves in place not only through a kind of structural transparency to the outdoors, but also through the inclusion of local materials and vernacular style — in each house, there is both memory and innovation.

One of the most effective ways Jim has found to marry the two has been to preserve and advance the element of craft in his projects. Using local materials and local labor, the designs and decorations produced through this craft approach are often as surprising as they are meaningful.

"I believe in modern architecture's simple elegance, but I also believe in decoration," Jim clarifies. "My hero is Frank Lloyd Wright and he had a passion for decoration that can strike the eye as very un-modern, but really it is a devotion to craft. The detail and particularity of decoration represent the kind of love and soul that we all crave in our lives."

Jim speaks enthusiastically of Wright's home in Arizona, Taliesin West, where the architect deployed utterly common local materials — concrete and native stone — to build an extraordinary and unique complex. What makes such a home modern, in his opinion, has mostly to do with its living qualities, its capacity to shelter and inspire its residents while connecting them to an ongoing history of place, to seasonal rhythms and shifting vistas.

Shelter and prospect. Jim's designs tend to keep their cards breasted, unfolding a little at a time into surprising spaces via transitions through confinement into openness, vernacular architecture into contemporary lines and volumes. He abides, in his own way, by Wright's edict, "The room within is the great fact about the building."

"There's a common mistake and I've made it before," Jim admits. "Basically, you spend it all upfront. You open the house with this massive great room, which amounts to a ton of unusable space, followed by your tiny bedrooms, tiny bathrooms, tiny kitchen, tiny garage. Then the house isn't just boring, it's unlivable."

For Jim, a livable home consists of a series of spaces where what is beautiful is what works. This has led him to a particular focus on points of connection as an important functional part of the house and an opportunity for conversational design. In his own projects, these moments of translation — from old spaces into new, from traditional materials into modern ones, and from vernacular into custom architecture — these are where the house lives and breathes, inviting residents to delight in the feeling of being uniquely at home.

"I've said before that free verse poetry is the hardest — so a glass house is hardest," Jim reflects. "In the sense that all the discipline must be self-supplied, that's true. But there are equally great challenges from working out of an established form. Form has resonances, cadences with a different kind of emotional impact."

Resonance and responsibility echo from the original structures, be they school, factory or farmhouse, which are the seeds of Jim's modern architecture. Within the demanding ethical, social and structural confines of this form, his attention to craft, to shelter and prospect, and to luxuriously simple spaces, has guided his inspired home building.

"I think an architect has the responsibility to keep learning," Jim asserts. "I think architecture is not like physics or mathematics. Even though it uses technology and engineering, it's an art. And because we live in buildings, work in buildings, even celebrate the spirit in buildings, architecture is a very human pursuit. It's in the humanities. It takes time to mature. There's a lot to be learned over a long career, which means an ongoing responsibility to keep learning how to do things better; to use technology better; to build things less expensively; to fit into the environment better."

Responsible for architecture in villages intimately connected to the Great Wall, a World Heritage site, Jim is committed to integrating his houses with the surrounding environment in ways that are both personal and political. His designs, often built with specific private clients in mind, are also a part of the life of the Wall, a structure of public importance. Issues of respectful development in close proximity to the Wall plague local residents and visitors, scholars and conservationists. Again, the balance is a tenuous one: too little development and visitors to the Wall will, as the mayor of Mutianyu observed, hardly pause to acknowledge the surrounding community; too much development and there's no community left.

Poorly sited and scaled buildings, plopped mere meters from the Great Wall, are not just a mark of disrespect for a historical monument; they also do significant damage to the delicate network of tree roots and ancient stone, which hold together the nearly 2,000-year-old barricade.

"Damage has been diverse," writes Great Wall scholar William Lindesay, who has spent decades exploring the wall. Lindesay has seen the Wall's capstones and bricks overturned to harvest the scorpions beneath — a new exotic food with high sale potential. He's also seen towers of all kinds surrounding and even built into the Wall, "to provide or improve reception for mobile phones and television."

As Lindesay recognizes, living respectfully and sustainably in the shadow of the Great Wall poses challenges to both newcomers and long-term residents. In the communities surrounding Mutianyu, for example, villagers are barred from selling wares at the tourist site — a privilege reserved for residents of Mutianyu Village alone. As a result, sharp differences in income and relationship with the Wall have cropped up among near-neighbors. In designing and building small businesses like the Brickyard Eco-Retreat in Beigou village, Jim and his partners have worked to address this issue by integrating visitors' conceptions of the Great Wall destination with the surrounding villages. There's a certain threading-together at work in each project. Each home or hotel room designed with an eye on the Great Wall is another built reminder that the place and the destination are one.

"There's too much that isn't excellent," Jim asserts. "The built environment should be beautiful! We come into a world so full of natural beauty, with so many distinct environments and landscapes. The architect, in fact each of us, has the responsibility to respect that, to build things that pay homage to the world we find ourselves in by recognizing and speaking to it."

Wall and *shanluan* layered mountain range, terraced orchard and tiled rooftop — Jim's designs are carefully articulated to speak to all that surrounds them. In building home, Jim has designed opportunities for private encounters with site. For example, views of the Wall, garden or cliff face can be seen from the shower. He has also designed for vistas from communal terrace and patio, public garden and pathway.

"Building home?" Jim asks himself the question and then speaks slowly. "My ideal when I work with a client is that when that individual first walks into their finished house, that he or she feels they've arrived home. These are bespoke residences, custom made for very special people. Now, can that same kind of concern for the people who will live in a space be expanded to include multiple people, multiple structures? I think to a certain degree it can."

Jim describes each client as a teacher. When he designed the hearth of his first commissioned home, the client reviewed the plans and said, "Well, Jim. This is very nice, but I know you can do better." It was a crucial moment. Jim not only redesigned and improved the fireplace, he began to enjoy the challenge of building with specific people in mind. Today, this approach, a kind of practical empathy in architecture, underlies his understanding of the social as site. Both client and community have taught him that home is at once a private dwelling and a structural member of a public fellowship, the built environment, which is home to the larger family of a community.

"One of the things that coming to live here really made me feel," Jim reflects, "was that I had never in my life, on a long-term basis, been part of a community. And what does that mean? Well, communities are first family-based and then neighbor-based. Growing up, I went to something like 10 different schools all over the US before I graduated from high school. I don't have any friends that I knew when I was 5, 10 or 15 years old. But you come to this village and people still know their friends from childhood. For the most part, they still live here. You may not be close, but here you have a sense of connection, of shared history. I never had that anywhere in my life — that is, until I came to this place. My heart is here, under the Great Wall. This is home."

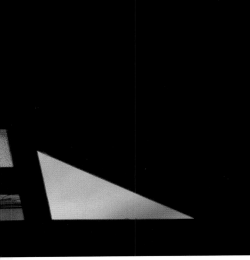

Acknowledgements

Early on in the process, Jim Spear sat me down to talk about the importance of writing oneself into a complex and collaborative project like *Great Wall Style*. I am still struck by the sheer generosity. A gift, because until that moment, the writing of this book still felt like wandering around a stranger's house at night. Already I was astounded — intimidated really — by the beauty of the houses Jim had built, many of which I had the pleasure of exploring during the course of this writing. I was awed by the images Robert and Ampol had captured of those spaces. What followed was an exhilarating, challenging and surprising process of discovery. Jim was extraordinarily generous in discussing his life and process, lending out books from his personal library, guiding me through the projects and introducing me to his many and varied influences — scholarly such as Matteo Ricci, literary like John McPhee, and architectural from East to West, from ancient to contemporary.

To become aware that each place and space is bound up in very human and deeply personal stories continues to be a gift. Thank you Jim, for trusting me to write my way into and through a project as exceptional as this one, for challenging me by example to grow and mature and produce nothing less than my best. Particular gratitude to you, Jim, for unfolding the meaning of home as a moving, illuminating story — one still in the making.

Stewart Wachs, mentor and friend, only a life committed to writing fine stories will do as a thank you for the countless hours you devoted to teaching me love of craft. Chronically deprived of sleep, you were witty and awake to word choice, texture and nuance; to rhythm, resonance and emphasis. You demanded clarity, focus and purpose in narrative voice. Thank you for introducing me to the subtle play between labor and inspiration and for encouraging me to write and keep writing.

Robert, Emily, Ampol and the whole collaborative team — I couldn't have asked for a more talented group of people to work with. Thank you to Liang Tang for tremendous care and generosity; and for teaching me, by the strength of your

convictions, about bravery. Julie Upton-Wang, thank you for wonderful stories and support. Gratitude to Zhong Wenkai, who brought an invaluable perspective to the discussion of material and space in this book. David Spindler and William Lindesay, wise men of the Great Wall, shared much about the life of that stone structure and the surrounding communities. Ronald Knapp's *Chinese Houses* introduced me to an entire history of shelter and was a pivotal influence and source for this text. Amy Lelyveld, member of the faculty of the Yale School of Architecture, gave the text an expert critique and provided the Foreword to this book, for which I'm tremendously grateful. To my Schoolhouse colleagues and fellow interns, family is the only word to describe such care, cooking and laughter — thank you. The Schoolhouse at Mutianyu Great Wall made this book possible, particularly with space and funds to work and publish. Many thanks to Condé Nast for letting us use some of Robert McLeod's first stunning pictures of the homes, shot for *Architectural Digest*. The publishing team at The Images Publishing Group — Paul Latham, Mandy Herbet, Alessina Brooks and many more — believed in this book when some of us were still just learning what it was, and helped us bring it to fruition.

Many Stateside mentors, friends and family are also part of this story. Ralph Savarese, who introduced me to creative nonfiction and forever changed my understanding of what an essay could be. Dean Bakopoulos, who reintroduced me to love of story and writing in community. My dear friends and family, the architecture of a life: Katy, Dani, Ben, Rachel, Jumi, Diane, Bronwen, Andi, Vicki, Song and my parents, Tricia and Tim. Mando and Whitney, who live on in the memory palace.

As with all worthwhile projects, more wonderful people than can be named here have breathed life into this book and inspired those who collaborated to create it. To those on these pages and those behind them, I am inexpressibly grateful. With you, I am home.

Team Members

Tessa Cheek
Author

Tessa Cheek graduated with a degree in Philosophy from Grinnell College, where she also edited the Arts section of the student newspaper, contributed to the campus literary magazine and won the James Hall Norman Aspiring Writer Award and the Selden Whitcomb Prize in Poetry. She worked in museum public relations before moving to Beigou Village to intern at The Schoolhouse and explore the meaning of home through the writing of *Great Wall Style*. Tessa is a regular essay contributor to the *Hypocrite Reader* and currently works as a reporter for *The Colorado Independent*.

Robert McLeod
Photographer

Serendipity, and a tip from a splendid hotel he was photographing in Beijing, led Robert McLeod and assistant photographer Poj Prommetta to The Schoolhouse for lunch after a visit to the Great Wall. Curious about the surrounding homes, McLeod requested a tour and was so delighted by what he saw that he shot a feature and pitched it to *Architectural Digest* himself. McLeod brought skills acquired in an illustrious career in architecture and design photography to capturing the intimate and evocative images for *Great Wall Style*.

Stewart Wachs
Editor/Mentor

Based in Japan, Stewart Wachs is director/chief editor of Heian-kyo Media, a division of the award-winning international quarterly *Kyoto Journal*, which he edited for 13 years. His writings have appeared on the Op-Ed page and Travel section of the *New York Times* and many other publications. Wachs has contributed to and edited numerous books and translations and also counsels authors. A tenured professor at Kyoto University of Foreign Studies, he teaches writing and writing-based courses. Wachs is also a photographer. His close friendship with Jim Spear dates back to the 1970s and he has visited Beijing and Mutianyu several times.

Emily Tang Spear
Additional Photography

Emily Tang Spear graduated with honors in Philosophy and Studio Art from Mills College. She would like to thank Robert and Ampol for the chance to participate in the photo shoots as an assistant and was honored to contribute images needed to fill out the book during the editing process. She has illustrated several books including "The Knitter" for children. Her hobbies and part time work include modeling, acting, and somatic arts. Emily was born and grew up bilingual and bicultural in Beijing, China. She currently lives and works in a Beigou village house repurposed as an art garage.

Ampol Paul J
Stylist

From Bangkok to New York, from Mumbai to The Maldives, Ampol is a global traveler who works as an interior decorator, event designer and photography stylist. He accompanied McLeod on his trips to Mutianyu and engaged the featured projects both respectfully and playfully in search of images that express the affective quality of each space.

Zhong Wenkai/SPACEWORK Architects
Architectural Drawing

Initially founded in New York in 2004, SPACEWORK Architects is now based in Beijing to fully engage the opportunities and challenges in China's dynamic process of urbanization. Zhong Wenkai is a partner at the firm and received his Master of Architecture degree from the University of California, Berkeley. Zhong is a friend and collaborator of Spear's. He collaborated on the Phase 2 rooms of the Brickyard and his case study of that project was published in the 2013/03 issue of *Time + Architecture*, the professional journal of the College of Architecture and Urban Planning at Tongji University.

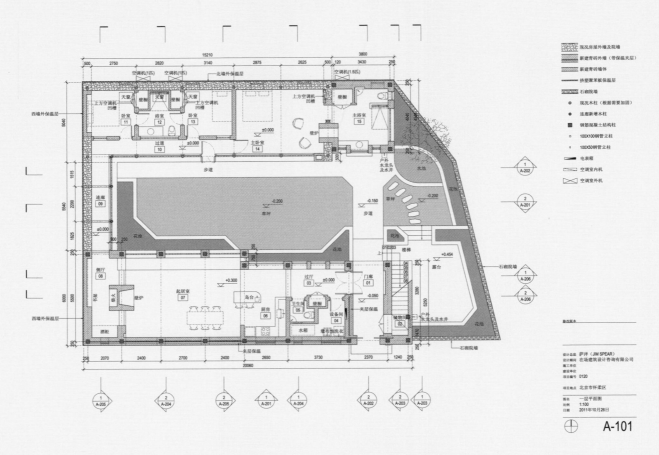

设计品名 萨洋（JIM SPEAR）
设计顾问 在场建筑设计咨询有限公司
施工单位
建设单位
项目编号 0120

项目地点 北京市怀柔区

图名 一层平面图
比例 1:100
日期 2011年10月26日

A-101

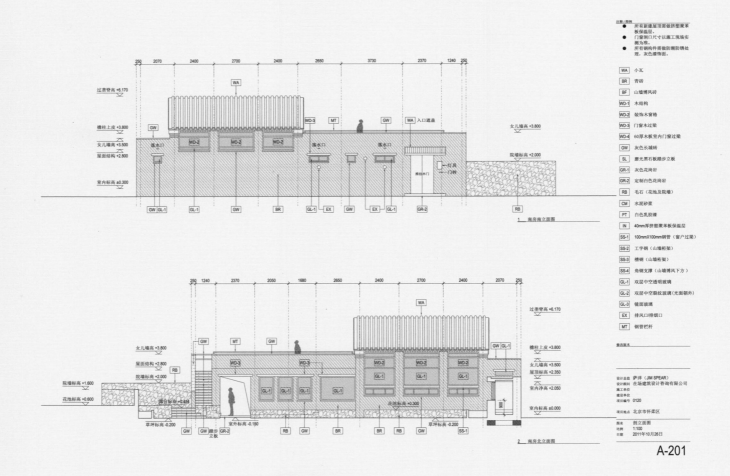

1 南房南立面图

2 南房北立面图

所有新建屋顶面做挤塑聚苯板保温层。
门窗洞口尺寸以施工现场实测为准。
所有钢构件需面做防潮防锈处理，灰色漆饰面。

WA	小瓦
BR	青砖
BF	山墙博风砖
WD-1	木结构
WD-2	装饰木窗格
WD-3	门窗木过梁
WD-4	60厚木板室内门过梁
GW	灰色长城砖
SL	磨光黑石板踏步板
GR-1	灰色花岗岩
GR-2	定制白色花岗岩
RB	毛石（花池及院墙）
CM	水泥砂浆
PT	白色乳胶漆
IN	40mm厚挤塑聚苯板保温层
SS-1	100mmX100mm钢管（窗户过梁）
SS-2	工字钢（山墙桁架）
SS-3	槽钢（山墙桁架）
SS-4	角钢支撑（山墙博风下方）
GL-1	双层中空透明玻璃
GL-2	双层中空裂纹玻璃(光面朝外)
GL-3	镜面玻璃
EX	排风口/排烟口
MT	钢管栏杆

设计品名 萨洋（JIM SPEAR）
设计顾问 在场建筑设计咨询有限公司
施工单位
建设单位
项目编号 0120

项目地点 北京市怀柔区

图名 剖立面图
比例 1:100
日期 2011年10月26日

A-201